THIS BOOK BELONGS TO:

_____

_____

_____

WHY DO PLANTS GROW?

Susan Horner
Illustrated by Nancy Munger

Moody Publishers
Chicago

ISBN: 1-8024-0921-0

1 3 5 7 9 10 8 6 4 2

Cover and internal design: Barbara Fisher / LeVan Fisher Design / barbfisher@earthlink.net
Internal design and production: Britt Menendez / bdesigns@sbcglobal.net

Printed in Italy

For my daughters
and all boys and girls everywhere in the world.
Each one of you is valuable, precious, and loved by God.

I give thanks for my husband and for each one of you (you know who you are) who prayed,
encouraged, or gave up your time to read and honestly share your thoughts.
You helped the idea become the books we now hold in our hands.

Special thanks to Michele Straubel and everyone at Moody Publishers
who had a part in this series.

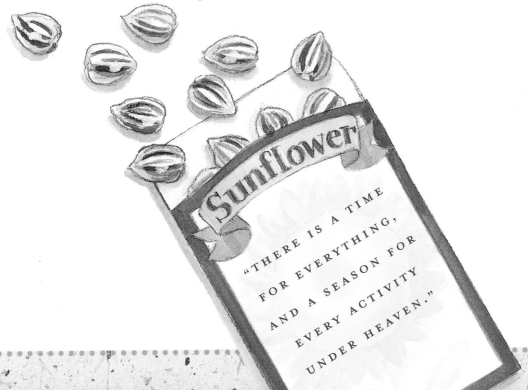

Sunflower

"THERE IS A TIME
FOR EVERYTHING,
AND A SEASON FOR
EVERY ACTIVITY
UNDER HEAVEN."

DEAR PARENTS,

I wrote the Miracle of Creation series because first impressions can last a lifetime. The word pictures we paint in our children's minds about sex and reproduction can influence their choices throughout their teen and adult lives.

Why Do Plants Grow? Why Do Birds Build Nests? and *What is God's Design for My Body?* build upon each previous book. All three books celebrate God's wise and good plan for His creation to reproduce in its proper season.

Why Do Plants Grow? and *Why Do Birds Build Nests?* are nature books. They will educate, edify, and gently prepare you and your child to discreetly talk about how babies are conceived and what biblical morality looks like in *What is God's Design for My Body?*

I wrote this book to help you relax and enjoy the beauty of God's creation with your child. I encourage you to look over the list of activities listed at the back of the book before you begin reading to your child. Our family had fun doing these activities, and I hope yours will too.

Don't feel any pressure to read this book at one sitting. In the spring and early summer, stop and take your son or daughter outside to watch bees pollinating flowers. Or close the book for a time while the two of you sprout a bean seed in a clear glass jar.

Let nature's reproductive ways gradually prepare your child to learn about biblical sexuality. For "There is a time for everything, and a season for every activity under heaven." The Bible tells us not to be overcome by evil, but to overcome evil with good. Our children are worth the time and effort it takes to sow good seed into their minds to help them overcome the negative influences all around them.

I offer you this book as a package of seeds. Just open it up, begin to read and sow, and ask God to make the good seeds grow. For one plants and another waters, but God gives the growth.

Blessings,
Susan Horner

Ecclesiastes 3:1 • Romans 12:21 • 1 Corinthians 3:6

pring! It's like a new beginning. Sleeping crocuses and daffodils wake up.
They push their shoots through the crumbly darkness to be greeted by
the sun and sky.

Breezes sweep through the lilacs, carrying their sweet smell through open windows, announcing, "Spring is here!"

Cherry and crab apple trees burst with color, while stately oaks quietly bloom and unfold their neatly wrapped leaves. Spring is the season for new life. Birds flit among the trees, building nests for their babies.

Spotted fawns on wobbly legs follow their mothers through the forest. Hungry mother bears wake up and lumber out of dark dens. Their furry little cubs skip alongside them. Spring and new babies are God's idea.

During the long winter, it's hard to believe the trees and bushes are really alive, that they are just resting and waiting. When we walk through brown bare gardens, we may wonder, *Will spring come back again?*

Yes, it will. The earth will again bring forth life, beauty, and color, because God, who set our planet in its orbit to give us time and seasons, has promised, "As long as the earth endures, seedtime and harvest, cold and heat, summer and winter, day and night will never cease."

It is God's plan to give us winter, spring, summer, and fall over and over again as long as the earth remains, for "There is a time for everything, and a season for every activity under heaven."

Just as the trees and bushes rest and wait, in my life and your life there are times of resting and waiting too: like having to go to sleep when you're not tired, having to wait to eat a candy bar until after you pay for it, or waiting to open a present you have wanted for a long, long time.

When has it been hard for you to wait?

Sometimes when we have to wait, we may wonder, *Does God really care about me?* Yes, He does. The Bible reminds us, "Trust in Him at all times, O people; pour out your hearts to him."

Seeds are good examples of resting and waiting. Seeds obey God's perfect laws of nature and flourish in their season. When God created the world, He made seeds on day three. He said, *Some seeds will make grain for more seeds. Other seeds will make fruit with seeds in it. Every seed will produce more of its own kind of plant.* And it happened! And God said it was good.

Psalm 62:8 • Genesis 8:22

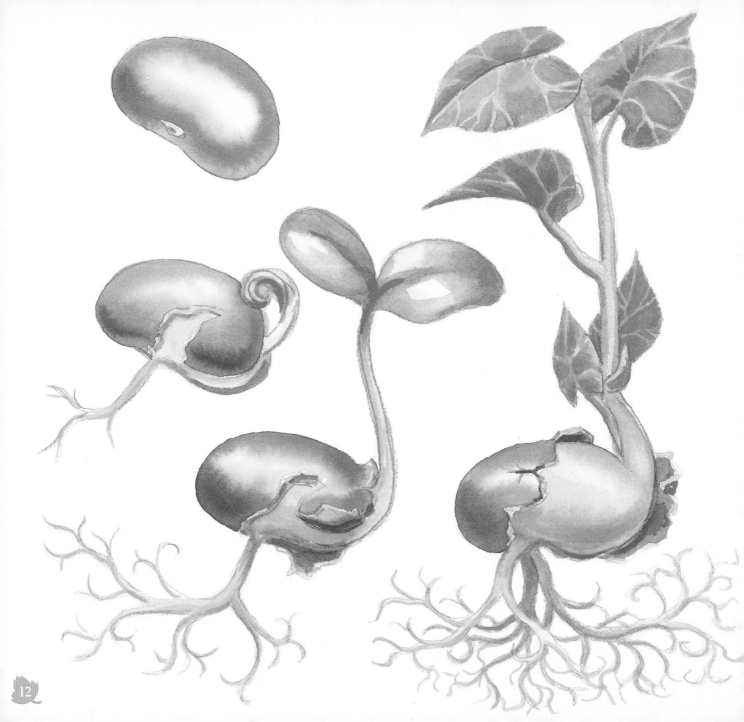

Seeds may look hard and dead on the outside. But living inside the hard seed coat is a teeny-tiny stem, a root, and a bud of tightly folded leaves surrounded by one or two seed leaves. All of this is within each seed you hold in your hand. The life within the seed is called an **embryo**. The seed's hard coat protects the embryo while it is in a season of resting and waiting.

Some seeds wait in packages on racks in grocery stores. Other seeds rest in the crumbly dirt of someone's garden in a busy city. Up in the high mountain meadows, and higher still on the mountain tundra, seeds sleep through the long winter under blankets of snow. Inside its jacket, each embryo rests and waits for just the right amount of water and warmth.

When spring returns, mountain snow melts into icy streams. Down in the valley, warm rain falls upon plowed fields. On the prairie and in the desert, the garden hose gurgles water to the awakening plants and seeds.

The embryo swells and pushes out of its softened wet coat. Its tiny root reaches down and grabs some crumbly soil. Its thin stem pushes up, up through the dirt.

The root then sends out feelers that work like straws, sucking in water for the thirsty seedling. The seed leaves feed the hungry seedling until its tiny true leaves unfold and soak up the sun's light. The stem continues to grow taller, and more leaves come out. Soon a bud appears. Its petals unfold and open for us to enjoy its scent and beauty.

Deep inside the flower is a sweet drink called **nectar**. Nectar is food for honeybees, butterflies, and hummingbirds who flutter among flowers and blossoming branches. While sipping sweet nectar, they do not know that they are carrying a powder called **pollen** to flowering plants and trees, so that next spring and summer there will be new blossoms and food for those who flutter by.

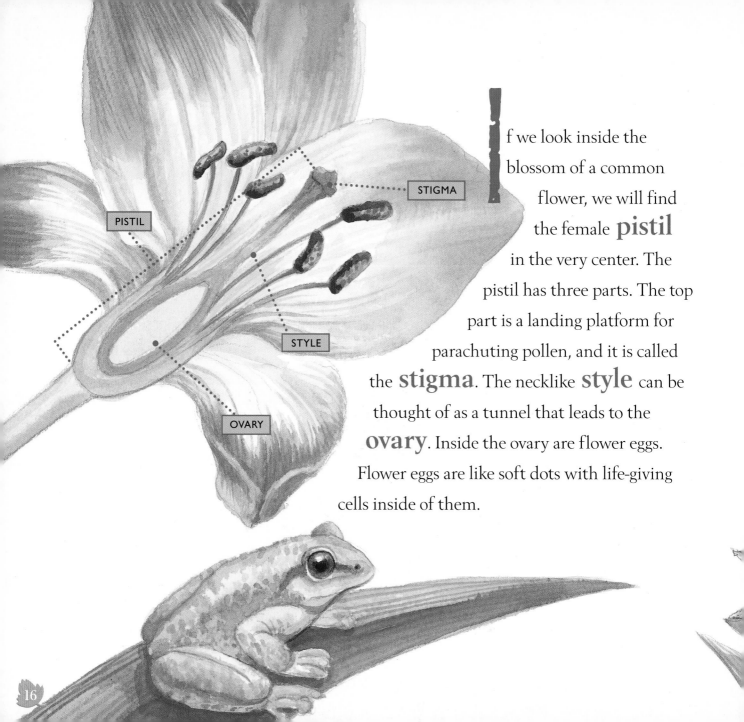

PISTIL

STIGMA

STYLE

OVARY

f we look inside the blossom of a common flower, we will find the female **pistil** in the very center. The pistil has three parts. The top part is a landing platform for parachuting pollen, and it is called the **stigma**. The necklike **style** can be thought of as a tunnel that leads to the **ovary**. Inside the ovary are flower eggs. Flower eggs are like soft dots with life-giving cells inside of them.

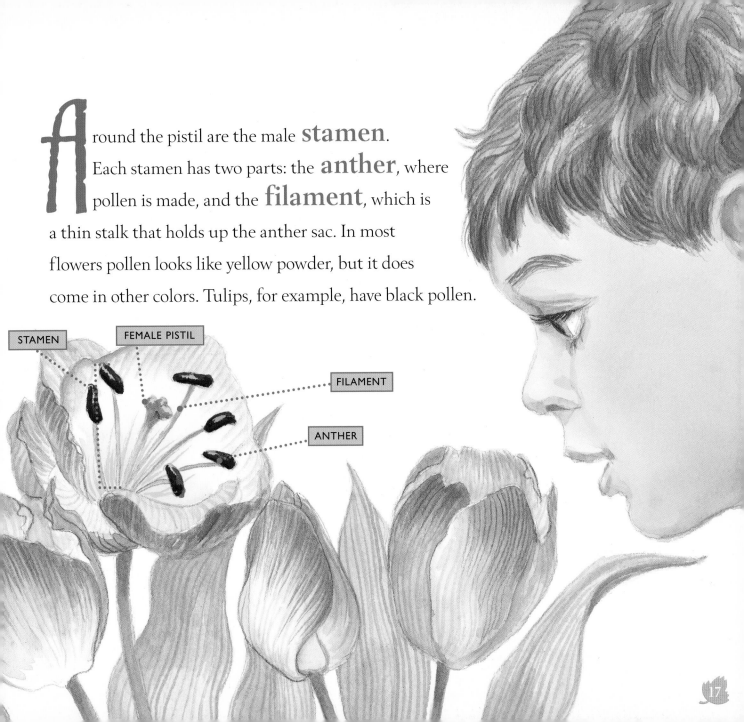

Around the pistil are the male **stamen**. Each stamen has two parts: the **anther**, where pollen is made, and the **filament**, which is a thin stalk that holds up the anther sac. In most flowers pollen looks like yellow powder, but it does come in other colors. Tulips, for example, have black pollen.

STAMEN

FEMALE PISTIL

FILAMENT

ANTHER

At exactly the right time the anthers open and the pollen granules slip out for a very important mission the Creator has given them to do. It is called **pollination**. The pollen will be lifted off the anthers and dropped onto stigma landing platforms in other flowers. The pollen may catch a ride with a bee, a hummingbird, or a moth. Amazingly, when the pollen is ready for its work, the landing platforms become sticky.

Bumblebees do not buzz around looking for someone to sting. They are out shopping for pollen to take home to their hives.

Watch a bumblebee collect pollen in her leg baskets, and then reach deep inside the flower to get a drink. Her furry body bumps the anther sacs, causing them to spill their yellow pollen. Then she flies to another flower. When she takes a sip of sweet nectar, some of the pollen will rub off the bumblebee and become stuck on the flower's sticky stigma.

A rose's sticky stigma juice will not have any effect on a violet's pollen. So if pollen from a violet lands on a rose's stigma, the pollen will not swell up like a sponge. Because in the beginning the Lord God made each flowering plant to reproduce after its own kind.

In flowering plants, a second sperm follows the first sperm down the tube and lands inside the egg just as the first sperm did. Inside the egg two special cells are waiting just for the second sperm. When the three of them join together, they grow into a layer of food. This food, called the endosperm, *is for the embryo. The seed's endosperm also provides oils and food for the birds, animals, and people on our planet who eat seeds and grains.*

Thanks to the bumblebee, the pollen has landed. The stigma's sticky juice causes each bit of pollen from the same kind of flower to swell the way a sponge swells up with water.

After a pollen swells up, a special tube grows down from it. The tube reaches down the tunnel-like style and comes into the ovary chamber. Inside the ovary are the teeny-tiny flower eggs. Each egg has a little door, and only one tube can come inside the door.

After a tube enters an egg, the male **sperm**, waiting up in the pollen, slides down the tube. At the end of its slide ride, the sperm lands inside the egg. Each sperm and egg carries half of what is needed to make a seed. When a pollen sperm enters a flower egg, we say the egg is **fertilized**, and it begins growing into a seed.

OVARY

SWOLLEN OVARY

The soft seed stays attached to the inside of the ovary. Messengers called **hormones** tell the ovary to swell up to protect and feed its tender growing seeds. That is how we get fruit. The blossom will fade away, while the seeds and fruit continue to grow.

God created each kind of flowering plant and tree with its own kind of fruit to protect its seeds and provide us with food. Even though we do not think of beans and pea pods as fruit, they really are. And so are tomatoes, cucumbers, peppers, and pumpkins.

After a season of being taken care of by the fruit, the seeds are ready to leave their protective home. Each seed's coat has grown hard to protect the sleeping embryo.

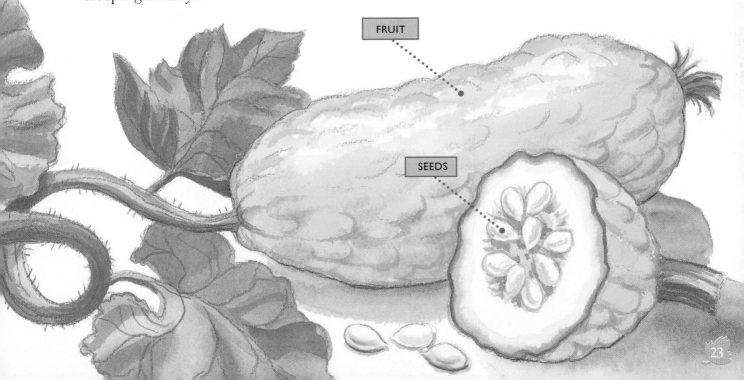

FRUIT

SEEDS

Different flowering families send out their seeds to start new plants on the earth in different ways. The ovaries of violets grow into seed pods. When the seeds are ready, the dry pods pop open, and the seeds fly in every direction.

The wild roses' ovaries swell into fruit called rose hips. Some birds and animals eat the fruit. The seeds travel inside their bodies. The seeds pass through the birds' and animals' bodies unharmed because of their protective seed coat. The following spring, a new wild rose grows far away from its parent plant.

Apples are picked from trees and sold in grocery stores, their seeds traveling with them.

Summer gives way to autumn with all its brilliant gold, red, and orange leaves. We look up when we hear calling geese fly over our heads. We listen for the sound of their wings as they move through the air. All too soon, winds turn cold, and trees stand leafless, while birds fly to warmer places.

We may feel sad when flowers dry up and are swept away with the wind. If we look closely at the dried stalks, we will see seeds, lots of tiny seeds. They are not dead; they are resting and waiting inside their hard coats.

When spring returns, seeds will break out of their jackets to color city gardens and high mountain meadows. They will brighten pastures, grow into orchards and golden fields of grain. Seeds declare the glory of God and show us that "There is a time for everything, and a season for every activity under heaven."

Ecclesiastes 3:1

FUN · FAMILY · ACTIVITIES

1. Take a bean and identify the seed's belly button. The indentation is from when the bean seed was growing inside the pod. Keep the seed wet in a white paper towel. Place it in a clear glass jar and watch it grow. Be sure to keep it moist at all times. Plant some other beans in dirt.

2. Take a stick of celery with leaves and place it in a jar of water. Add a few drops of food coloring. After an hour, observe the celery. See how the celery stalk draws up the water to its leaves. You can also do this activity by using a natural white carnation.

3. Plant pumpkin or zucchini seeds. Watch them grow. Children may enjoy making sketches or taking pictures of its growth. After the plant flowers, identify the female and male parts. Take a cotton swab and pollinate the flower. Talk about the wonder and beauty of God's plan to use sperm and egg for the earth to bring forth beautiful flowers and enormous trees. God has given fruit two jobs: one is to care for seeds, and the other is to provide food for animals, birds, and people.

4. Take pollen from different flowering plants and look at it under a microscope. You will be able to observe that each species, or kind, has its own shape and size.

5. Shop for indoor blooming amaryllis bulbs in the fall and winter. You can find them at a plant nursery. Be sure the plant has light. Start watering it and watch

your bulb grow. When the bulb blooms, help your child identify the male and female parts. When the stigma becomes sticky, use a cotton swab or toothpick to lift some pollen from the anthers and place on the sticky stigma. Continue to water the plant after the flower petals dry up. If fertilization took place, you will be able to observe the ovary swell. Eventually it will pop open and you shall see the seeds.

6. Memorize Bible verses together. (You may find it easier to learn these two verses by heart if you make up a tune to go with them.)

Ecclesiastes 3:1
"There is a time for everything, and a
season for every activity under heaven."

Psalm 62:8
"Trust in Him at all times, O people;
pour out your hearts to him, for God is our refuge."

For the second verse, fill a plastic pitcher with water. Allow each child to hold the pitcher by himself or herself and pour the water. (You may want to do this outside or over the bathtub.) Say, "As you pour out the water, tell God whatever you want to say to Him. You don't have to say it out loud; He hears your thoughts."

7. Read a biography of Johnny Appleseed.

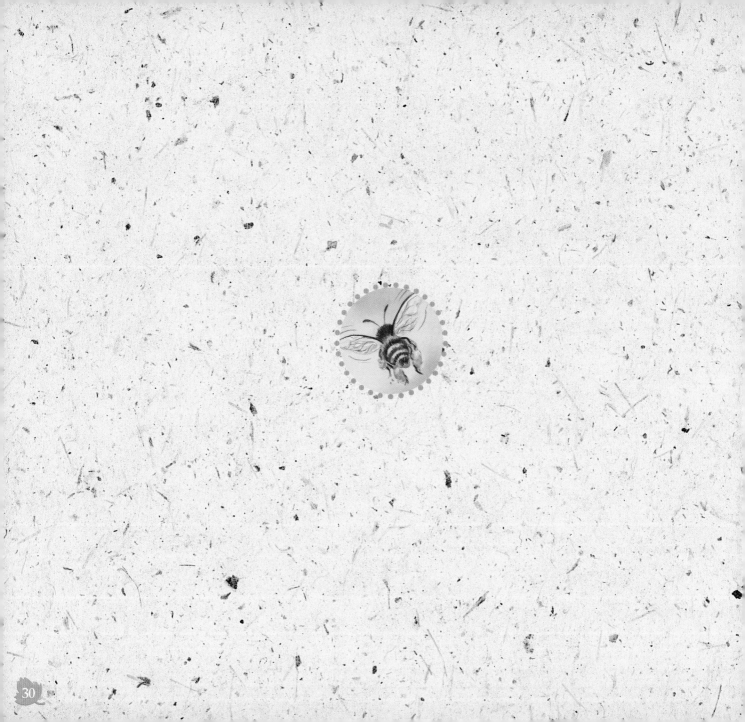

GLOSSARY

anther: The part of the male stamen that produces pollen.

embryo: The tiny life found within a seed.

endosperm: A layer of food used by the embryo inside a seed.

fertilized: A flower egg that has joined with a sperm cell from the pollen and will now grow into a seed.

filament: The thin stalk that holds up the anther.

hormones: Hormones are chemical messengers.

nectar: A sweet drink made by flowers that is enjoyed by insects, bees, hummingbirds, and small animals.

ovary: The part of a flower that holds tiny flower eggs, which grow into seeds after they are fertilized.

pistil: The female part of a flower, made of a stigma, a style, and an ovary.

pollen: A powder produced by the anther, in the male part of a flower.

pollination: The movement of pollen from the anther of one flower to the stigma of another flower.

sperm: A tiny cell from inside the pollen that joins with a flower egg to create a new seed.

stamen: The male part of a flower, made of an anther and a filament.

stigma: The part of the female pistil that becomes sticky to catch pollen.

style: The necklike tunnel that leads from a flower's stigma to the ovary.

Since 1894, Moody Publishers has been dedicated to equip and motivate people to advance the cause of Christ by publishing evangelical Christian literature and other media for all ages, around the world. Because we are a ministry of the Moody Bible Institute of Chicago, a portion of the proceeds from the sale of this book go to train the next generation of Christian leaders.

If we may serve you in any way in your spiritual journey toward understanding Christ and the Christian life, please contact us at www.moodypublishers.com.

"All Scripture is God-breathed and is useful for teaching, rebuking, correcting and training in righteousness, so that the man of God may be thoroughly equipped for every good work."
—2 TIMOTHY 3:16, 17

MOODY
PUBLISHERS

THE NAME YOU CAN TRUST®